DSLR
Portrait Photography

Abhishek Ghosh

DEDICATION

Everyone dedicates the authored book towards own family. I am no
exception.

CONTENTS

PREFACE BY DR. ABHISHEK GHOSH

Despite most of us own a digital camera, a computer and an inkjet printer at our homes, many of us still visit the nearby studio even just for an official photograph. This book possibly can not convert the reader to a full fledged professional portrait photographer but the tricks can help the reader a lot in real life.

Without taking some risks, without the smaller sufferings, none on this Earth has ever been successful to create something or to learn any new skill. Mastering an art is not really fully under the control of the learner. Portrait photography, among all the niches of Photography, is the oldest niche and it is not really possible to avoid this niche - it is a demand for our day to day needs – starting from the need to have a digital photograph for an online profile to showing one's own fiancé's photograph to an aged online friend who has been virtually a relative with time.

This book has been named as DSLR Portrait Photography - this never means, a Mobile Phone Camera user can not use some of the tips written within this book. A camera really can not take Photography, this book only can help the person behind the camera.

One can read while having a good Mobile Camera or Point and Shoot camera, grasp the basics and understand the bottleneck - cost of the equipments for the ownership and needed upgrades for a DSLR Camera. In essence, a DSLR Camera is not an automated machine to take great photographs.

Today a high end DSLR Camera is truly the digital version of our traditional SLR camera, there are some definite pros and cons of the entry level to mid range cameras, if compared side by side with a full frame or medium format DSLR. Current trend has made the DSLR Camera a consumer grade product – unfortunately, a SLR Camera never a consumer product. The DSLR Camera will remain as a prosumer product.

A typical good point and shoot camera can give the best return of investment to most of the users - yes, Author should think about the readers more than the DSLR Camera manufacturers. This book can be helpful decision making guide to acquire a new DSLR camera or upgrade from any existing camera. It is not uncommon to find the frustrated DSLR Camera owners confused by description of numerous costly accessories on various online writings.

Really, there is no shortcut to master the art, specially if the user has near zero idea about traditional drawing and painting. With the penetration of digital camera, Portrait photography has been opened up more for experimental opportunities due to a big factor – reduction of the maintenance cost, which was normal for the film cameras; purchasing the film, developing and printing were burdens and hinderances to the learning curve. The standard film negative's size was 35 mm, which in DSLR world is equivalent to a full frame DSLR. A good full frame DSLR costs quite higher - the total cost of ownership actually has been increased. May be, one might be interested to experiment with the Digital Backs.

The cost of the lenses and other accessories has not been decreased that much. If the reader calculate the cost of a standard notebook computer like a 15" Mac Book Pro with Retina Display, hardware equipments to calibrate the display, the needed professional post processing software (read Adobe Photoshop) - total cost of ownership has been increased much more than Film Photography. Definitely a Linux computer running GIMP can serve the purpose of post processing reducing the total cost of ownership but still yet, free softwares are not yet the standard for graphical works unlike virtualization, cloud computing softwares where free softwares are the standard. What we have gained as the end user is the easy to experiment with shots. Cost per shot has been decreased to almost nil, if we compare with Film SLR cameras.

Still, photography never means equipments. Portrait Photography can more be experimented by a photographer in this era of Digital Photography due to reduction of cost per shot plus the ability to check the result instantly. This book is written taking the fact granted, the reader owns a full frame DSLR at minimum. Readers using DSLR with APC size sensor, should be aware about the added optical distortions, cropping factors for mounting the mentioned lens in within this book for the purpose of portrait photography. Author of this book do not recommend to mount lens of focal length lesser than 50mm on a DSLR body with APC size sensor in order to keep the cropping and optical distortions under control. To reduce the total cost of ownership, the reader must define his/her preferred niche of photography.

1 INTRODUCTION

The importance of this book starts from the inherited pros and cons of a typical entry level to mid range DSLR Camera. Currently, there are good number of nice books on Digital Photography, be they are specific for the Portrait Photography niche or cover all the topics of Photography. This book and the Author of this book has no aim to deny their credibility. Some of them should be read to learn more and understand how one should progress to improve skill. This book is more inclined towards the short and effective articles published on blogs.

Over 60% of the user today, unfortunately buy a DSLR either imagining that a DSLR camera itself has a magical capability to increase the quality of photograph, this imagination is attributed for the huge promotive misleading Ads by the manufacturers or going with the buying "another gizmo" trend. Just like, a Mac Book Pro can not make one to learn UNIX, a DSLR Camera can not the photography better. This book is highly suggested to be read both by the new DSLR owners with limited experience or future DSLR Camera owners. Even a mobile device user who never used a film DSLR, can apply some of tricks written in this book to get the best out of the camera.

What ever the reason was behind the purchase of the current DSLR, may be the reader falls among the rest 40%, who at least have the wish to learn or are already trying to learn, this book can prevent the common pathetic ending - selling the DSLR at Ebay or some other easy to sell online website – this fate is really quite common and applicable to both electric guitar and DSLR camera. Any need, related to this book, can be requested directly to the Author of this book via e-mail to admin@thecustomizewindows.com or simply one can point towards Author's popular technology blog – thecustomizewindows.com. Author is committed for additional support to the readers by publishing articles to clear any topic which is not clear. Furthermore, there is existent support dedicated for this book on Facebook and Google Plus Pages for reader's quick enquiry.

Nowadays, most of the standard blog writers, after a time becomes the Author of standard printed Books from good publishers. The reason is not for earning a quick money, indeed writing and printing a book is not really easy and a secured way to earn money, if ever compared to a blog. The reason is to provide a printed kind of manual to the readers. Reading on computer is not really like reading a printed book.

Readers are suggested not to skip any chapter of this book or read the chapters in a random fashion.

If the reader has purchased the book from Amazon store, we highly recommend to do an useful review for the future buyers. May be, the book fails to meet the need of the reader. Instead of providing a one star review (which actually can not return the money you invested), you can contact the Author and provide a feedback. We appreciate readers' feedback to make this book better in the future Editions.

So far, we can summarize what we want to say in just few points :

1. Without really having a DSLR, anyone can buy this book or even borrow from your friend and apply the methods on existing camera.

2. Learning a new skill is always hard

3. There is a slight difference between a traditional Film SLR and a DSLR camera – a top up knowledge is required for the existing Film DSLR camera users

4. Free unlimited online help is bundled with this book for lifetime.

Portrait Photography is a genre where a range of artistic initiatives revolves around the idea of showing the physical or emotional mood of the person or persons through the photos. Portrait Photography is not only important for personal collection or as a part of family album, Portrait Photography is needed in official documentations including print media, press releases, author bibliography etcetera usages.

Mostly a Candid Portrait Photograph is considered to be the standard for being a good Portrait Photography of a person. Before Digital Photography penetrated en mass, Portrait Photography was equivalent to either a facial photograph taken inside a studio setup or taken by a professional. But with the penetration of technology, the chance of experimentation has been increased, Portrait Photography has itself taken a sharp bend towards being more artistic.

Hit-or-miss chance for adding optical artistic effect like bokeh is present more now, specially in outdoor or for so called social Portrait Photography. The reasons are simple, with a small viewfinder on Film SLR, it was difficult to estimate a very small area in the background. Development from Negative Film to an image took few hours with own setup, which was in the later phase mostly replaced by digital reproduction of images from negatives and needed bigger machines.

Specially the introduction of low cost Prime Lens yet acceptable reproducibility, like Canon EF 50mm f/1.8, made a big change in Portrait Photography for the DSLR users. This factors become apparent if one searches for portrait photos in any Photography related websites like deviant Art or Flickr or may be some online forums.

With time, the once most important requirement of Portrait Photography, a soft focus lens, has been reduced due to very good quality image editors like Adobe Photoshop.

In our old film cameras the images were recorded on a photosensitive film and subsequently revealed by a chemical process, but in DSLR the images are captured by an electronic sensor that has multiple photosensitive units, which take advantage of the photoelectric effect to convert light into a signal power, which is digitized and stored the memory.

The resolution of a 35 mm film is about 320 pixels per inch – approximately about 87 megapixels. The quality of a film camera in the hand of an expert said to outperform not only for megapixel count, but also for not having the artifacts added by digital photography system -noise. As it is not a physics class, we will go straightforwardly to the advantages and disadvantages of a DSLR.

Clear cut advantages of a DSLR :

1. DSLR can show the real image to be taken.

2. Parallax error is less, the real image of the composition can be determined.
3. The AF mechanism to be used as the phase difference AF can continue to follow it precisely, even when shooting motion.

Clear cut disadvantages of a DSLR :

1. DSLR is a heavy weighed camera.
2. As there are lot of mechanical movements, capturing an image produces typical sound of shutter, which might be problematic for certain conditions.
3. A set of lens is required for different range of focus.

A DSLR is not a camera for all. Not even a DSLR makes to take 'better images' without knowing about photography. A DSLR is an advanced camera for those who needs or loves photography. Be it Portrait or any other niche.

Portraits can be divided from the point of setup – a portrait can be taken inside a studio or outside.

2 LENS FOR PORTRAIT

Portrait Lens is the photographic lens, which are perfect for taking artistic portraits. It is more easy to pickup the wrong Lens due to various reasons. We are not going to discuss the elementary chapters on Photography taking that the reader is already used to these topics either by reading our blog or and standard blog or book. So, practically choosing a good book and reading Author's active blogs on the Photography Section on thecustomizewindows.com is quite important; the reader can directly communicate citing his/her book to get a helpful hand. The reader must know the minimum about Rule of Thirds, Golden Section, Crop Factor like basic topics.

There is probably no Lens which can be stamped as The Portrait Lens. This idea of Portrait Lens arrives due to various reasons. A factor should be kept in mind, a DSLR equipped with a APS-C sized Sensor and a DSLR equipped with a Full frame sized Sensor are not exactly the same from optical point of view. With certain lenses, optical complexities can get increased when mounted on a Medium Format DSLR.

Prime lens with typical focal length 50 mm and 85 mm and wider opening are traditionally known as portrait lens. Portraits seem to be very natural when we are working from a distance in a range arbitrarily about of three meters or a bit more; at such a distance, which is normal considering everyday interaction with other peoples in real life. For a full-format portrait photo this results in a angle of about 15° to 30°, which is considerably smaller than the optical angle of a typical standard lenses − which is about 45° to 55°. Foot zoom is always great over complex zoom lenses. Standard lenses may well succeed taking good portrait photos, wide-angle lenses are unsuitable for classical portraiture, since the working distance for a frame-filling portrait is very small and it leads to a strong distortion ("moon face" or big nose error). Cropping and blurring the restless background with more short lenses is difficult or near impossible in the post processing step.

In the area of film SLR cameras (with a small format 36 x 24 mm film) typical portrait lenses had a focal length of about 80 to 135 mm. In this range of focal length, the presentation is perceived as a pleasant distortion, but not flat. While the smaller sensors of digital SLR cameras in accordance with the form factor demands a shorter focal length lens for Portrait Photography. So, for a Digital SLR sporting with a APS-C sized sensor, a lens with lesser focal length will be required for the reproduction of classical portraiture.

An important composition option for the portrait is a shallow depth of field. For this purpose, large aperture is necessary with usually an initial aperture of 1:2.8 or faster, there are lenses available with an initial aperture up to 1:1.2. At maximum aperture, the face or the whole person can be isolated from the background and foreground – fully optically. Some lenses for portrait photography is known to have a soft focus – Minolta Varisoft is a classic example.

Of course one can use the supplied kit lens, which is essentially a zoom lens; it can also help to create a nice portrait photograph. Kit lenses are built and packed to the customers to make the offer more palatable – not one of these lenses, no matter which vendor is really worthy or can take the advantages of their camera to the fullest. Usually for Canon DSLR users with APS-C sized sensor, the 50 mm f / 1.8 (Nifty Fifty) is a basic suggested Prime Lens. f/1.4 with the same focal length is definitely a big deal if you compare the price of 50mm f/1.2 Lens.

Nikkor has similar range of Lens like that of Canon. Full frame cameras have a much shallower depth of field which is a big advantage for portrait photography, simply because the subject, can more easily be separated from the background. Prime Lens in general are preferable over a zoom lens for portrait photography. As we are not taking about the techniques of Portrait but only the Lens; this much is enough covering the normal need of knowledge.

3 CAMERA MODES

Which camera mode the reader should choose depending on the situation? This is really like as if taking the person who is learning to drive a car from the solitary driving practice place to the real world. Now, one really can not increase or decrease the luminance of the Sun at wish. Rather, one should target to capture the reality in an artistic way.

The aperture priority mode allows the user to manage the aperture, the camera will manage itself automatically according to the speed. Like all priority modes, the user must select the sensitivity before. The opening or closing of the diaphragm can manage depth of field, so the user can play with the depth of field. But, when to use a large or a small depth of field ? Rather, when to use a larger aperture ? More one opens the aperture, the depth of field becomes smaller, it means that the resultant depth of field can be expected to be very short or shallow. On a standard lens (50mm) at f/1.8 on a subject about 1m, the net area will be between 1.10m and 1.20m, just for an example. This mode is used a lot in portrait photography and in macro - to get to the blurred background. It is great if the reader wants to isolate an object or an element from it's environment. In which case the user will almost close the diaphragm? The more one opens the diaphragm, the depth of field becomes smaller as said above. Conversely, in landscape for example, all the objects in the frame must look sharp. Be careful, even in low light or on a cloudy days, a tripod may be necessary to get the best result. With a small aperture (f/22 for example), the exposure time can drop low enough to compensate the exposure.

The shutter priority mode lets the reader choose the shutter speed or exposure time, the other factor, the aperture, in this scenario then get managed itself. The reader can choose the sensitivity, as like in aperture priority mode. The longer it stays open, light enters the (camera's) sensitive surface. The setting becomes difficult when the reader will have or need a movement to shoot - according to it's speed, also depending on the lighting conditions. The shutter priority mode allows to capture the movements without risking with ending up with a blurred subject which is moving too fast. In sports photography, it is often used because it can isolate the movement. Thus, the photo against a speed of 1/800s is chosen so that the subject remains in focus despite the relative speed. Recall basics of Physics - relative speed, camera plus the user and the subject - all are actually moving to certain extent!

However, a lower speed should be chosen to create a motion effect and to simulate the impression of speed. In such cases, the reader can use a monopod. Slow speed is often used in landscape photography to create a "fuzzy" effect on the flowing water – seas, rivers, streams. Using a tripod is essential in such cases, because it is in excess of the second and the slightest movement of would create a bad "blur". This is basic, there are other ways to obtain the effect. The reason to describe flowing water has relationship with Portrait Photography. Two set of shots can be taken for a Portrait and the knowledge, creativity can be mixed on Post Processing to get a surreal effect.

Program mode allows the user to keep manual control on some settings, such as sensitivity, like over / under exposure or white balance. However, the device determines the correct shutter speed / aperture lens, so that the user can not not have all the freedom might want. This mode is a good way to begin to understand the initial setup, the sensitivity is a pretty important factor for the quality of the reader's creations, including the amount of digital noise present on the photograph. Unfortunately, in Film Photography, kind of equivalent of "digital noise" used to throw an artistic effect.

Other two modes are Automatic and Manual. Manual should be used or rather must be used after a good practice and unless there is hurry. Manual mode obviously the best for full control on the camera, which is typically absent in Point and Shoot and High end mobile cameras. Possibly this mode is one of the reasons to purchase a Digital SLR.

Rest remains to explain is the auto mode. Auto mode practically is kind of mode where the DSLR becomes like a point and shoot camera – the result obviously is not great because everything is determined by the camera. There are some brand specific modes like Sport mode, portrait, etceteras, they are merely extensions of Auto mode and do not give access to any settings. Unfortunately, Auto Mode of DSLR can produce horrible results when compared to a Point and Shoot camera. Depending on Auto Mode is one of the most common reason to get fastruated with DSLR Camera. This paradoxical phenomenon happens as the firmware (that is the software which drives the camera) uses mere fuzzy logics like a washing machine. DSLR Camera, yet can not be configured for Machine Learning.

4 MASTERING PHOTOGRAPHY

Fortunately enough, there are some shortcuts, which can be stamped as Key Points. Some key points exists to master the portrait photography to get a closeup photograph of the face of a person as it should be – natural. What basically an average user wants, is a quite easy way and possibly improve portrait photography skill to prevent the photographs from becoming disappointing. These key points to master the portrait photography niche has certain dimensions, which needed to be analyzed. If the reader is not sure what the basics of photography basically is mandatory need to know and probably what need not to know, improvement is quite difficult to achieve.

Key points to master the portrait photography can be divided in to three parts – first part is already discussed in the above paragraph – that is, to prevent from becoming fully ruined by applying the basic rules of Photography like Golden Section, Rule of Thirds etceteras; second part is what is said in this chapter and last part practically already read by the reader in the previous chapter - What Camera Mode to Choose Depending on the Situation.

Since the face is usually used as a kind of marketing tool or as a trade mark of a human (pun intended), it must reflect the personality of the subject, without being forced. As a photographer, it is up to the reader, how to capture the subject in order to make it enjoyable and give a natural appearance. There are many ways to take a nice close-up, using different types of lighting.

Do not forget the body

It is easy to forget the pose of the body, because it also influences the photograph. For example, if a person is leaning forward, will also tend to lower the neck and head. It can unfortunately magnify some undesired "natural beauty" of the subject, like double chin! This theory is true for all the mammals - we can not rotate our head to 180 degrees in horizontal plane and our head is usually at 0 degree relative to spine in vertical plane. The reader can think about a bird (avian, not a mammalian) to make the theory clear. As we are not performing a research on complex anthropology, we can simply remember - leaning forward can make a photograph funny, which possibly is not desired in most serious scenarios. One might be thoughtful about fess furry animals like a dog, actually they have shorter necks. More furry, adorable mammalians like nice looking rabbits or Author's fiancé gives us an extra plus point - the hair really can do a great work. Although, the function - Author's fiancé does not exist at the time of publication of this book!

Stretch and approach

In this case the corners are very important. That is said, hold the camera at eye level of the subject. Definitely, it will reproduce a picture which is more spontaneous and natural.

To optimize the position of the face the reader can ask the person to raise the head upward a bit, to stretch the neck to certain extent. Also the subject can be asked to push the face towards the camera, to further stretch the neck and stretch the skin of the face – about an inch will suffice.
It is a great trick to remove the wrinkles, expression lines and make the skin more toned. But make sure to provide clear instructions, many times people tend to carry forward only the chin or forehead. If it happens, ask them to bring the nose towards the camera! One should be careful about the sleek young girls with short hairs while applying this hypothesis.

No Distractions

Forget props or backdrops extravagant. A photographer possibly will want the attention concentrated on the face, not on an object in the background or a landscape. It is not surprising that why many professional photographers take close-ups on white background.

Not all depends on the light

But, as with any photo, the right lighting can make a big difference. Avoid using too much light which is hard. Spread the light with a panel, make it bounced on a wall, use a soft box, one should choose the preferred method after experimentation, but it is not recommended to point the flash directly at the subject. Whatever is the wish, it is mandatory to have the softly diffused light falling on the face. A light on the hair will give further prominence to the image, separating the head from the background.

Do not force the subject

It is essential to take the expression as natural as possible. Instead of asking the subject to smile, one should make sure to naturally bring the smile involving the subject with conversation. Keeping talking about something that interests them or sharing few jokes can ease the situation.

The jaw line

Apart from the eyes, the other area of focus is the jaw line. It is the one element that gives shape to the face and one should make sure to photograph it from the right angle.

Distortion is not your friend

One can use a telephoto lens and step away from the subject. Then zoom in on the face. Shooting with a wide-angle lens will give the face a little pleasant distortion, it might be just what the reader is trying to avoid! Normal Lens and/or Fixed Focal Lens are obviously the best for the purpose of portrait photography.

5 TIPS TO IMPROVE PHOTOGRAPHY

Tips to improve portrait photo from being disappointing is probably desired by the most readers and photographs that contain people, on average; make more appealing to the others. We often find ourselves in situations where our photos include people as major elements : moments of everyday life, special events or purely portraits. When we are beginner photographers or if we still need to learn how to shoot portraits more better, it is quite easy to get disappointing results from our first attempts. Fortunately, there are a few simple tips, which can be applied in most situations, that put us on the track to achieve the best photographic portraits. These are basic concepts, but they make a big difference. Many of the elements that make a good photo, as well as the composition, the choice of subject, the choice of the light, the choice of the environment, remain in the hands of the photographer.

Eyes on fire

In the vast majority of cases, less than the artistic experiments, the eyes of the person to be portrayed will have to be in focus. Normally, the human figures in a photo attract the attention of the observer and within the human figure are the crux are the eyes. If the reader have a camera system with multi point focus, author will suggest to place the point of focus to the eyes. If we fail to do it, then we have changed the frame to some other place from the point of focus - on the eyes. Half-press the shutter button and then recompose, without approaching or moving away from the subject in the meantime. Beware of the fact that, autofocus mode automatically decide the point of focus : it can not focus where we want from our normal sense. Also be careful when we use an wide opening - a very wide aperture. Wider opening is desired for blurred background, an opening too wide at a very close distance may lead to an excessive portion of blurred image and a greater difficulty in having eyes perfectly in focus. So - in essence, there is a virtual limit of wider opening for Portraits. Weigh this point against our chapter on Lens for Portraits.

Telephoto Lens, yes, thank you

The focal length recommended by some photographers for portrait is 85 mm. Others climb up, reaching even 200 mm. There is no focal length perfect for portraits. What is true is that, generally; it is best to choose focal lengths above 70 mm. This becomes more true as we get closer to the subject being photographed - foot zoom. There are two main reasons behind this choice of focal length : longer the focal length goes toward the wider angle, more the subject is distorted, for example by extending the nose and making the inter distance of two eyes going more, longer the focal length is high, more is the desired to be reduced part of the background of the photograph is included, increasing the importance we give to the person to be portrayed.

Be intimate

A mistake we made often during our first photographs, we do not get close enough to the subject to be photographed. It happened instead of reading the advice to get closer to the subjects of their photos, to be more intimate. In portrait photography, what is even more true is, since a shorter distance is of major importance to the to be photographed subject, actually it creates a sense of intimacy even to the viewer of the photo.

Wider opening

As noted above, a wide aperture can cause difficulty in focusing, but it is also a common feature needed to be used in many portraits. As we have discussed in tis book so far, a wider aperture allows the photographer to isolate the subject in focus in a better way. Usually, this is the result we want to achieve in our portrait photographs. A good aperture value can be f 2.8 and below and then with a larger aperture, risk of incurring the above problems (especially if we are very close to the face of the person framed), above the background becomes less blurred and then we lose the insulation.

Give attention to the background

The eye and the human brain exclude the portion of the scene on which the attention is not needed to be focused, but the camera is not so smart. We must always be careful, what is the background – so as not to spoil a photo otherwise would be successful. This is also true in general. For portraits, in particular, two basic recommendations are : the horizon, if present, must not cut the neck of the human subject, the photographer have to pay attention to objects which are aligned with the subject, while avoiding to create strange effects – such as a branch sticking out from behind the head to make artificial horns. To implement these two recommendations, it is usually necessary to change the perspective, rotating around the subject or changing the height of our point of view.

These tips can make a difference in many situations. One should try to put them into practice.

6 TIPS TO IMPROVE COMPOSITION

This chapter to improve the composition in portraits is of completely different flavor - When we are going to take the pictures of peoples, there are some simple rules of composition that we can apply to avoid the trivial errors, which would be annoying to those who are viewing the picture and also, they add interest to our shots to make them looking more professional.

Remember the rule of thirds

The rule of thirds is a very simple rule, but for a beginner can lead to a big improvement in the composition. It applies to all kinds of photography, so one should not forget about it is a scenario for portrait photography. In particular, as pointed out in previous chapter, in most cases, the major focus will are the eyes, so one should make sure to align the eyes to one of the intersecting points in the rule of thirds.

Point of view

The tone of the picture changes a lot depending on the point of view of the photographer than the subject. Framing the person from the top down or from the bottom up, we can get different effects, we can highlight the physical characteristics so that it does not like to stress the negative points – such as a broad forehead and a prominent nose. So, if one just took a picture that does not convince us – the viewers and the reader can not identify the reason for dissatisfaction, one should try to photograph from other points of view and compare the different results. Experimenting with other points of view can add dynamism or even humor to the portraits.

Vertical orientation

Most of the pictures are taken holding the camera horizontally, portraits get a more professional look when the picture is taken holding the camera vertically. Not for anything else, the vertical orientation itself is called "portrait orientation" ! This advice is applicable where the photographer is running for a very close portrait, which only frames the face, that is a full-length portrait. This does not mean, however, that a portrait photo taken in landscape orientation is not good.

Leave a space to look at

In many portraits, the subject looks straight into the lens. When this does not happen, it may be a good idea to a leave space in the direction that is of the look of the subject. This means that, if the subject is looking to the right, we will make sure to leave some free space in the frame on the right.

Do not chop out disproportionately

When certain body parts of the frame are not included, they must be "cut" carefully. In particular, three main aspects are to be taken into consideration : avoid 'cutting' the fingers or toes, better completely exclude hands or feet; if the limbs are cut exactly at the height of the joints it will create a feeling of a disorder of the subject in the photograph, so better to cut at an equal distance from two joints; if the reader look sat many of the shots, in the fashion industry for example, will find that a very common technique is - cutting the top part of the head.

Fill the frame

As in the case of the rule of thirds, this is another good advice in many areas of photography. To give importance to the person to be portrayed; expression should be present to involve the viewer of the photo; to reduce the weight of the background, it is better to try to fill the frame as much as possible. In particular, it is better not to leave excessive space above the head of the person to be portrayed (which goes hand in hand with the example of common practice in fashion industry).

7 COMMUNICATING WITH THE SUBJECT

Portrait Photography is an art. Portrait Photography is itself one the reason of the niche's long success. Portrait Photography measures a Photographer's various skills. Today we can not imagine a World without photography. But there was a day, when people in core business were thoughtful about the success of Photography. If Photography was not made popular, the companies would see no profit and the technology would have not been progressed. It was the Portrait Photography, which was used a tool to "catch clients". Like today Apple makes your head dizzy with various looks and features in their Ads, Photography was also promoted in that way to get a market. Number of books, articles, techniques still far exceeds for Portrait Photography than any other sect of Photography. The basic reason is – some takes great Portrait Photography but most eventually fails. Most fails to take good Portrait Photography of their mother, wife and daughters! There are reasons why the failure rate with closer females are higher.

In fact, the natural expression and pose that distinguishes a successful portrait has nothing to do with aperture and exposure time! It is directly influenced by the relationship between the Photographer and the subject to be photographed. Unfortunately, the transition to digital photography has changed some aspects, as many photographers as professionals have adopted the strategy of shooting endlessly to do a lot of pictures to try to get some usable from the "pile". A matter of statistical fact. That sometimes, it must be said, gives acceptable results, but does not go beyond this point.

There are two distinct categories of Photographers. Professional and Amateur. Amateurs will not require many points which are must for the professionals. The reader might arrive with a broken hand to to the Author crying like a kid, if the Author of this book starts to cry with genuine emotion, it will not look quite professional. This attitude makes a big difference with an Intern and an experienced surgeon.

Universally it is taken granted that a professional attitude should be a kind of neutral attitude. Some overdoes it, ending up to an unsuccessful drama, while some can make it a real non scripted drama. Where one will start and stop has normal social limits. Touching an unknown female unnecessarily can invite blows.

The reason to mention these practical points is for a good reminder - Portrait Photography can be a challenge to anyone. If the photographer is a young male and the model is a young female and none is present except these two humans in the room, the situation is not quite easy in any country. It demands an eye to eye contact. It is better to envision the person with some relationship specifically for the starters. Older females can easily be mother like. Younger is not much of problem. Younger definitely not means a 25 years good looking single female. There is no country or place in this World where eye to eye contact does not make a young male a bit apprehensive about own reputation. Its true for any creatures – eye to eye contact is one of the closest non verbal contact. Thankfully enough, a camera has a viewfinder to hide the eyes like a shy girl.

If a young male photographer is too much shy, the female model will also feel uncomfortable (unless she is really 'very easy going' with any kind of males, possibly it does not point towards a good character or may be state of mind!). If she is uncomfortable, the portrait will reflect the attitude. Treating the relationship professionally, is the best way, since it not only allows to obtain images which are far more effective but also it adds a value of as a photographer and as a person. It begins well before taking the camera in hand. Author personally feel comfortable to talk with a young unknown girl in office or OT but feels very much uncomfortable in a shopping mall. If it was the reverse, that was abnormal. The tools of trade make us comfortable.

Even if it is exactly known, whom to be photographed, it is advisable not to immediately take the camera in hand but let the other speak, photographer should ask and listen carefully. It is advisable to try to predispose the individual to be relaxed, put at ease in any way, even with a trivial thing like offering something to drink as per norm of the society one lives.

One should not let the long silences make over but speak almost constantly. And it should be done in accordance to the proper manners: if the reader is doing a close-up in a room and the subject is within two meters range from the reader, it is advisable to avoid using a commanding voice or tone. Conversely speaking almost in a whisper, also helps to create a more intimate relationship. We will suggest not to try to do anything what the reader is not like. There is enough chance - will be overdoing.

One can talk about a computer or a flower vase, it is an art to understand what the other person is used with. If the reader has requested a particularly complex pose to the subject, be sure to do a few shots and then let the subject rest for a few seconds before resuming the same pose. Tiring the person to be portrayed by forcing exceedingly is not recommended. If the reader is a male, it is advisable to avoid unintentional, spontaneously touches to a female without asking her, particular if the reader want to touch the hair to adjust. For these uncomfortable situations, talking about mother's habits, wife or girlfriend's habits can ease the ways.

If the model is female and has an accompanying mammalian like husband or boyfriend, the reader's work is to impress that person towards self; a smallest tint can spoil everything. Females will try to fly away, this is a natural phenomenon. They will never surrender so easily than you can think. The reason to mention these points is – there are innocent peoples, who get in to trouble without knowing what the he / she did the wrong.

8 CAPTURING GENUINE EMOTION

Capture genuine emotions in portraits ensures that the composition is interesting, the desired portion of the face is in focus and adequate lighting is present. At one level, these things become easy, but that is not always so easy is to capture the emotions – that is Candid Photography.

If the reader is used with portraits on regular basis, it is sure to have some informal checklist to, at least mentally, which as a photographer the reader executes both before and after pressing the shutter button. One need to ensure that the composition is interesting, the desired portion of the face is in focus and adequate lighting is present for the subject, all the important things, to be sure. At one level, these things become easy, but is not always so easy is to capture the emotions. From street photography to spontaneous portraits, it is very difficult to capture the genuine emotion with an aware subject, because the photographer is going to record the moments calculating they might happen in future, there is a benefit from unawareness or indifference towards the camera.

But when it comes to pose for a portrait session, getting the genuine emotion from the subject can be a difficult journey. Many people normally tend to tense up while arrive in front of the camera. At the other extreme, many reacts with exaggerated smiles or any kind of facial expression that is unpredictable and unflattering. It takes a bit of effort – mostly when one decide to be a photographer simply aware – but make sure that the subjects express certain emotions spontaneously - it is certainly an achievable goal and has huge profit. Consider the following tips apply if portraits are formal or follow the impulse of the moment, by profession or hobby.

Words, words, words

Chat or chirp, however one wants to call it – this is especially important if the person the reader is shooting is a stranger. Talking helps the photographer, to get an idea about the personality of the subject and helps the subject to forget the camera. One can ease by asking questions about him/her, without being obtrusive or get too personal, but expressing a real interest in the answers. With someone unknown the reader, it is natural that one may run the risk to talk on a topic that the person is not ready to discuss, so the ways can be - talking with moderation and making sure that they dictate the flow of conversation, taking cues from their words. Also, one can tell a funny story to bring a natural laugher or smile. No matter which approach one uses as a photographer, one needs a certain degree of intuition, more nicely one can apply, the better results one will get.

How to use the environment

Suppose the reader is shooting in the studio, not in a home (or a friend's home). But have the wish to do some portraits in the living room, some in the bedroom, some in the back yard. But before starting to change the scenarios within the house, it is advisable to start with the easiest setting, allowing the person to feel comfortable with the reader and the camera. People tend to feel comfortable with their favorite things and they love to show them, especially in the context of a photograph.

Becoming a director for the better results

Not everyone will feel comfortable with orders. But one should try to see oneself as a sort of wise and enlightened person for guidance, which guides the subject in the right direction. Allowing them to know before the instruction - which way to tilt the head, where to put the hands, where to look and anything else that can bring out the best. The subject will feel under an expert guidance, all remains relaxed to pose. No matter what facial expression the reader want to get, these tricks always work.

Using the element of surprise

We have already established that people have a tendency to become embarrassed when the camera is pointed at them. This will not be true for all, but it is inevitable that one as a photographer will have to deal with this situation, sooner or later. Deceiving to doing something unrelated to camera can make the subject distracted. These special moments when the subject does not feel the weight of the lens, probably by acting in a more natural way, may provide some golden opportunities. The spontaneity of these shots can reveal the genuine emotion that a photographer usually seeks for.

9 POINT OF VIEW

Point of View Shot is a terminology which simply means a way one need to photograph to force the viewer to make fell as if the subject is looking through the camera. Let us explore how we can the theory in Portrait. By now, we have covered most of the theoretical part of Portrait Photography. Camera Angle has direct relationship to the subject. Usage of point of view shot in Portrait Photography is rare – usage of Point of View Shot more in Cinematography. In practice, it is possible to use Point of View Shot method for better composition or rather for achieving a wider array of dynamics.

Point of View Shot or simply p.o.v. is when the camera take the shot from a particular person's viewpoint, as if the person, who is watching; is the person who is looking to the person in focus in that portrait. To explain it with an example – two persons, one is the reader's friend, second person is the Author and the third person is the reader, who is the photographer – here the reader is playing both the role of photographer and viewer. If the reader take a shot of the friend's face while Author is in conversation with the friend standing face to face – the reader will compose the scene in a way so that, right side of the composition will have a blurred portion of Author's head and shoulder as foreground.

Actually, it is quite commonly used in motion pictures to simulate "reality". What has been described here is known as over-the-shoulder shot. When the leading actor is the subject of the POV it is known as the subjective viewpoint. A subjective attitude is often one of the two directly successive settings : one shot shows a character who looks out somewhere, usually on a point outside the image. The other option (the actual POV shot) shows what the figure considered, filmed by the position of the figure.

Filmmaking is quite difficult – it is few thousand time difficult than taking a great photograph – a minor mistake can turn it to a fully "home made video". In real life, the example situation is quite common or just can set up it to simulate as if it is a candid.

Point of View Shot brings an illusion, i.e., the viewer feel like an insider in the composition. Often POV shots are technically alienated : Blur signals about the look of a spectacle wearer without glasses. The subjectification (a philosophical concept coined by Michel Foucault) of the POV shots is often contradictory combined with an objectification through technical devices, such as the view through telescopes or night vision devices. Both increase the impression of authenticity.

The tone of the picture changes a lot depending on the point of view of the photographer than the subject. Framing the person from top to bottom or from bottom to top matters to highlight the physical characteristics such as a broad forehead and a prominent nose. So, if a picture taken does not convince us and does not identify the reason, we should try to take pictures from other points of view and compare the different results. The ranking of the canonical line of sight of the photographer is exactly perpendicular to the subject. Experimenting with other points of view can add dynamism to the picture or even humor.

An old mother is having conversation with his young son, along with taking the mother's usual portrait, a Point of View Shot can spice up their family album. Dramatic moments of life – wedding, death, birth of a child can be excellent natural moments to use this theoretical model. What lens to choose? Usually a Normal Lens or a Wide Angle Lens will work fine!

10 CHOOSING POSES

Tips on choosing poses for stunning portraits brings great set of ideas needed for Portrait Photography. In the previous chapters, important points on composition, choose the right equipment has been discussed. Yet, the subjects still do not appear as they would like to appear. If the quality can not enhanced, they always seem to be a bit out of the place. The presence of human subjects is both the strength and at the same time is the difficulty in a portrait. Even the most beautiful person, if it is not comfortable in front of the lens or poses wrongly - can never be photogenic. A good point to start with is capturing the portraits of strangers, which is taken milestone to learn photography.

Even when working with a professional model, directing the subject in order to obtain the best pose is primarily the photographer's responsibility. These tips on choosing poses might not be the last word, but definitely they will work. On this topic, on the Internet there are multitudes of articles with generous advice. In this chapter we are listing the most significant ones. Using them alone or in combination will allow the reader to identify the effective way for choosing the subjects, regardless of their size, their shyness, the purpose of the picture.

Head and Face

Head and face are definitely the most important elements in a portrait, no matter how much of the frame is – that is why it is portrait !

The head tilted slightly backwards suggests a sense of challenge

Head bent toward the high shoulder creates a sense of fun and winking (more suitable for women)

Head bent down towards the shoulder and is lower expresses power

Turning gaze away from the lens moves the focus to another object or to create a sense of mystery and tension when this item is not framed

Look to the lens creates a contact, but adds intrigue and challenge

It is better that the shadows is directed to the primary light source

To have the "twinkle" in the eye, do not lower your chin too (depending on the direction of light)

The face must not be rotated so much as to protrude from the line of the cheek

If one eye is hidden due to the rotation of the face, it is better that it is completely hidden rather than visible in half

When there is more than one person, does not align the heads at the same height

To avoid the double chin, better push the chin forward

Arms and hands

The hands, after the face, attract the viewers' eye too much, here are the tips to portray them correctly.

For men, generally it is better that the hands slightly closed, as if clutching a large stone

For women, best is outstretched fingers

Thumbs in pockets with hands on (own) hips express safety and strength

Hands in his pockets give a casual appearance

Generally it is better that your hands are relaxed

For lateral shots hands should be positioned so as to be laterally framed avoiding to frame directly the back

Holding an object to hold in hand or placing on a surface on often help to create a more natural pose

Bent elbows bent give a sense of comfortable informality

On the contrary, straight arms are very formal and often better to avoid

The arms better be spaced from the body

Never bend the arms at 90°

Do not to photograph naked armpit

Torso

The posture and rotation of the torso affect the overall tone of the pose and the aesthetic qualities of the subject.

Turning the chest slightly makes the figure appear more slender

Even if the subject does not need to look more slender, generally it is better not to have the chest perfectly perpendicular to the lens

Women can highlight the line of the breast slightly arching the shoulders back

It is better to have one shoulder higher than the other, by rotating the torso or bending the arms

The shoulders aligned exactly to expresses the strength, is not suitable for a woman

It is absolutely necessary to always have the back straight; not too rigid, but a proper posture

Legs

If the subject has legs within the frame, the position of the legs helps a lot to control the entire posture and also make it to look overall slim and slender.

Putting one foot forward, reduces the apparent circumference of the thighs

Feet, as wide as your shoulders give impression of strength

Generally it is better to have one leg bent

Shifting the weight on back foot helps to have a good posture.

General Notes

Some considerations for overall appearance.

In general, the joints must be folded, must not remain straight and rigid

The subject should sit comfortably and be informal

Also a vertical surface (wall or tree) helps to lean in this direction

Leaning slightly toward the camera on the subject suggests interest and involvement

Instead of bending towards the subject, one can photograph slightly from above

It is better cover the arms with cloths as it would take away attention to the face

Expressions

Best are the natural expressions, no forcing should be applied

Subject should not smile in every photo, in many cases, relaxing the face is a better solution

When the subject smiles, must not forget to smile with eyes

A subject who is interested himself/herself can try to play with the expressions, but the risk of ridiculous faces is always lurking.

Duties of the photographer

There are also a bit of things that the reader can do before and during the photo session to ensure a better result.

Photographer have to be with the subject, a chat to understand their expectations and personality

Find the most appropriate location for the type of shooting and for the type of subject

One can also pay close attention to the light at the venue; if necessary, set the scene (like a stage)

After having posed the subject, allowing a break to pose to capture a more natural gesture

If there is more than one person present, photographer can get help in distracting the subjects, respecting the wishes and difficulties of the subjects

Testing some pose in motion: jumping, racing can help to identify unexpected beauties.

11 AMBIENT LIGHT IN PORTRAIT

Ambient light in portraits is extremely useful to make a leap in quality to the portraits. Evaluating the best possible usage of light is crucial for portrait photography, as well as for any other type of photography. Normally, there is a definite need to photograph the situations that normally occurs in everyday life or for example, the reader is beginning photography and yet has not ventured in buying an external flash, in such situations, almost always the photographer have to use the ambient light.

The sources of light that a photographer may have can be divided into two large families:

Ambient light, which includes all kinds of light freely available in the environments, may be the sun outdoors, but can also be a lamp inside a house; artificial light sources which are appropriately positioned and set as the flash attached to the camera, one or more flash suitably positioned and activated at a distance, and other specialized lamps of various types.

Choosing placing, setting up the artificial lights in the proper way is a daunting task that requires extensive experience and advanced knowledge. Moreover, it is not always possible to have multiple flash or lamps or the time and space to arrange them correctly. Moreover, to obtaining the equipments can be quite expensive. There are also professional photographers who specialize in the use of only the ambient light for portraits. We will present to you a few tips, some tricks, to take the advantage of the ambient light only when photographing people.

Many believe instinctively that the optimum light is under the sun in the middle of the day. This is not true for landscapes and perhaps is even less for portraits. This type of light has at least three large main shortcomings:

Flattens the colors, reducing the saturation
Casts very dark and too harsh shadows which are unsightly on the face and the body of the people
Often forces to grimace and squeeze of eyes to protect from the sun – which is not really what is photogenic.

The soft light of a cloudy day, when shooting outdoors during the day, the hint for many is to seek a place in the shade, such as under a tree or in the shady side of a house or choose days when the sky is covered with cloud. If then we really have to stay under the sun, we try to make our subject to wear a hat. The reader will easily find that in these cases the light is much better. The main reason is that the direct sunlight is directed precisely, while when we are in the shade or under the clouds, the light is diffused and reflected is so much softer. This type of light is perfect for many kinds of pictures and in particular is very precisely indicated for portraits. Similarly, if we are in and we want to take advantage of the light coming from a window, we use the curtains or an opaque tarpaulin on the glass.

In addition to ensuring the quality of light, one need to observe carefully the direction from which the light comes. If the previous method has been applied, the light will come mainly from the bottom, then the ground and sideways, for example because it is reflected from a wall. If the reader performs some experiment, will notice that the light at the sides, especially if it hits the face of the subject to be photographed at an angle of about 45 degrees, easily provides a result - which is very pleasant. At this point, the question arises : how do to make sure the correct angle of the ambient light ? Fortunately, the solution is very simple : as the light can not be moved, the subject have to be moved.

Sometimes it will be sufficient to rotate the head towards the right or towards the left or bend slightly, sometimes just moving to another location will suffice. The same theory can be applied if the photo is taken from inside. If the light is coming from a window, it is needed to make sure that the subject is sitting with the cheek turned toward the window. If instead artificial lights is used, it is better to prefer the lights which we can move, much easier to handle than a chandelier hanging from the ceiling, of course. In real it would be much more complex, but this is a good starting point to begin to get a nice ambient light in portraits and from there starting to experiment begins.

To understand this chapter it is essential that to learn the minimum on the mode of exposure metering. Since in a portrait, of course, emphasis is given to the person framed, it is crucial that this last point is exposed perfectly. Therefore, many recommend to use the spot metering mode (or alternatively weighted center) and to measure the exposure of an area of exposed skin. This means, in the spot metering, moving the point of focus, is one in which the exposure will be measured, on the face of the subject. But if the center-weighted metering is used, it is necessary to move the subject in the frame and then eventually lock the exposure (via button AE-L).

12 STUDIO PORTRAIT

Once, Studio Portrait Photo was the mainstream of Portrait Photography. Digital Photography gives the opportunity for a Studio setup at home – Studio Portrait Photo in own Setup or rather Studio Portrait Photography. The ideal setup is actually somewhat like a bigger Light box. It operates on the basic laws of Physics on behavior of light rays. The incident light should be diffused and the reflections should be uniform within the area where the model will be. As it is practically not possible to make a room sized Light Box, reflectors can be used and so as other diffusing materials, including drapes to make the environment.

The model will sit about 2.5 m in front of the background. A flash from the front, left at 45° to the model in about 2.0 m hight, 1.40 m distance from the face will be placed. It must be flashed indirectly, so the light is reflected on a white screen, a 200 Watts studio flash, with 100% power. A flash from the front, on the right: 45° to the model in about 2.0 m hight, 1.40 m distance from the face will also be needed. It will be flashed indirectly, the light will be reflected on a white screen, the studio flash power is again 200 Watts, with 50% power.

A hair light or continuous light or beauty light usually set with honeycomb from behind and above, aligned relative centered behind the model in case of females. A white styrofoam plate, held by model herself can serves to reduce the shadow nose or chin shadow.

If the reader is fully new to DSLR or have never used Film SLR, it is likely to get terrified with the description written above. The reason the setup has been discussed - a studio setup provides an excellent opportunity to practice with various semi-automatic or manual modes of a DSLR camera.

Back to the topic, the person must be photographed from slightly from above. Another good position to shoot is at the eye level, which is always flattering for the model, rather than to shoot from below. Obviously a tripod will be needed.

The ideal focal length for portraits is 80 mm, equivalent to the medium format (equivalent to 50mm with crop factor 1.6), since this focal length is the closest to the human visual system. Reader can also use longer focal length, focal lengths below 80 mm, equivalent to the medium format (equivalent to 50mm with crop factor 1.6). Exposure may be kept at ISO 100, manual mode should be used, with a fixed timing with 1/60 sec. The correct exposure is done using an external light meter. Its value is determined and adjusted manually on the camera.

There are obviously more points, but this is the basic setup. If the reader has lot of faces in own house, there is not much to think for. These setups are great to comfortably take photograph. DIY Photography Studio Setup is not costly. One can have a DIY Photography Studio at home if approximately 300 USD is spent. How decent it is to do some experiment with food photography, still life, portraits with artificial light, toy photography.The Bare Necessities for a DIY Photography Studio Setup at Home :

1. External flash
2. Stand for the flash head
3. Umbrella diffuser
4. Cable release to control the remote flash
5. Soft white non reflective fabric sheets

Definitely, the non-studio portraits are day to day demand. The whole book, indeed is on non-studio portrait! For the entry level DSLR cameras, specially on fully new hand, the DIY studio setup helps a lot than one can imagine.

The main light is the one that which determines the overall effect of the image, all other lights should scale. It is said that the light is more powerful, but it certainly is the most important, as it is entrusted with the task of illuminating the most interesting part of the subject. The effect created by artificial lights must resemble as much as possible the perception that we have with natural light. The sun casts shadows of an individual in one direction and also in the photo studio, to achieve a natural effect, you should try to have only one shadow casting near and two shadows or more are perceived as unnatural and not only become unsightly, but they are a real nuisance. The lighting of the sun always comes from above and casts its shadow in the lower part of the subject, then laterally, at 45 ° to the vertical axis of the subject, things lighted in this way will always be perceived by the eye as natural.

The biggest yet not really cared fact the reader will need to master with a studio setup is the effects of lights – we actually can reproduce or simulate various lighting situations with control. In real life, we have less control on the natural lighting effects. Charity begins at home. Car driving is best to learn at a solitary place! The points which we will learn with a new DSLR, with zero experience of SLR camera handing, with this 'trial-setup' are :

1. Handling of the DSLR
2. Holding the DSLR properly
3. Getting used with not looking at the controls while shooting
4. Looking through the viewfinder not the screen
5. Understanding your own height with respect to an average human and the required adjustments of your posture with the camera – increasing the skill of balance
6. Neck-strap is ugly but mandatory part of any type of SLR camera.
7. Quickly changing the lens

Soon, the typical shyness, uneasiness of using a new device will go away with more practice.

13 SELF PORTRAIT

Self Portrait can push creativity to the next level, even with a mobile phone camera, but how one can manage the flow ?

Probably because you know yourself better, may be you do not have a model to practice, may be you do not have the person who know at which angle you will look better. Most importantly, you can be the most free with you than anyone with in this World. If you do mistake with your Self Portrait shots, be it technical or anything, you will yourself see it first. Digital Photography has made Self Portrait more easy. Even a good mobile phone camera can take a good Self Portrait, the catch point for any point and shoot or mobile phone camera is – you need to know the weak points of the camera's very well. In general, the noise becomes very prominent in mobile phone camera which you can solve with illumination somewhat in the way we do in studio; a bigger DIY Light Box might be impossible for this purpose if you are not a small creature but you can actually use multiple umbrella's and white light source for soft illumination, a post processing becomes mandatory (you can check our step by step guide for post processing a photograph taken by a mobile phone camera in Adobe Photoshop).

Many takes Self Portrait that looks pretty identical to the others. Creative ideas must be present for a Self Portrait, making it closer to Candid. If you use Mirror for Self Portrait, do not forget to again reverse it by either using Mirroring feature on the camera (if available) or edit in later on computer as a part of Post Processing. You will probably not love to see you left sided things on right side – most misses it on Mirror shot Self

Portrait photograph because I or you, can not see ourselves in real. May be as we are fortunately a symmetrical thing except our parting line of hair. Probably none has one sided mustache.

Regarding the technical part of taking a Self Portrait, a tripod will allow you to keep the same frame on a series without tiring to hold the camera at an arm's length. I am fatigued with seeing hundreds of left arm (which is, in real is the uncorrected right arm) Self Portrait Photographs on deviantArt. Alternatives for a tripod can be to find a support – wall, table, dressing table, but you will have less choice in the positioning of your camera. Self Timer or Remote is an indispensable part of Self Portrait photography.

You can use the autofocus of your camera, but be sure that you are on a plain background. Another pitfall, is the focus on another object rather than you. Easy trick is to lock the focus at your eyes. We actually notice the eyes in most Self Portrait. The worst thing about human face is (unless you are a stage performer) is the chin's position – in Self Portrait often the chin tilts a bit up (because you are trying to do a hard thing) making the face towards a bit fat.

If you are a male, on average all type of pose might work (either clean shave or do not shave for at least 3-4 days, in between might produce pathetic result), but if you are a female, there are some artistic rules those are applicable to Self Portrait. Female's sketch can be drawn by few arcs. If an arc becomes triangle, it becomes odd looking – example is elevating the shoulder in most common poses.

14 CANDID PHOTOGRAPHY

Candid Photography and Digital Camera has a good relationship on the basis that, with a digital SLR the photographer can take multiple shots without any extra cost. Digital Camera by quality is on compromise when compared with a traditional film SLR, but two factors – the virtually absent incurring cost like buying films and the ability to transfer them on computer instantly, has made Digital Camera more acceptable. As human beings become aware of a camera's presence, the awareness abolishes the normal expressions which can be noticed seen normally and often a person's signature attitude. Candid Photography is taking a person's photograph without making the person (s) aware of presence of Camera. So, by definition, all photographs of a child, up to the point when the child is not aware of camera or photography is actually a Candid Photography.

Candid Photography has a difference with photographs taken by professional photographers including photojournalists for capturing a person's / persons' decisive moments, emotional moments etc. In case of Candid Photography, the permission is actually given – for example, if you are taking photograph of your mother, busy in the kitchen, the permission is not actually needed as morally, socially and legally it is taken that, you will not abuse it – like selling it and not offering the photographed person the share of revenue.

As because of huge misuse, taking photograph of non relatives, without permission in many countries can amount to quite serious crime if complained, beware of taking photos of others without permission for sake of creating an art named Candid Photography. This includes, in most of the countries, taking photographs of boyfriend of girlfriend, if the other complains, as because possibly no one signs a legal contract or agreement for such relationship. Most importantly, a third party can complain against a Candid Photography taken by you where the person's permission was not taken. Reader should be aware of rules and regulations of own country.

Basically there is no specified standard rules or standard definition of Candid Photography. It is taken taken that from general consensus, the camera will be a DSLR or equivalent with good suitable Lens like a Prime Lens of appropriate focal length. The reason behind this general consensus is, due to difference among the camera, its optical components and skill of the photographer, a photograph can be a Candid Photography or just a snapshot photography. Effects like Bokeh are usually present in Candid Photography. Candid Photography has no standard as it can be faked – situation can be setup with proper photographic arrangement.

15 PORTRAIT OF STRANGERS

Portraits of Strangers is a theme that is more varied and interesting. Billions of individuals, each with unique characteristics, similar yet have unique expressions. The images that portray the ways, expressions the individuals pose as we begin to dream, expression, feelings and distant memories which end up within oneself, the most intense emotions are vivid. Yet many photographers, even among professionals, do not approach (or do so only marginally) in this universe of possibilities because it requires an additional step that goes beyond the knowledge of the instruments and photographic techniques; a new element not in the sleeve of new shiny and full frame : interacting with a person.

The reasons for avoiding Portraits of Strangers are usually two : the atavistic fear of rejection, possibility of receiving no answer for a polite question to take a photograph and in the event the contrary, if the new photographer got a positive reply, do not know how to handle a subject, - what to say, how to say; a whole host of similar concerns that afflict the mind. These distract the photographer many times by the technical aspect with the result of not paying attention to other aspects such as framing, focus, exposure. To defeat that little voice inside that hinders the new photographer, that mantra of "but I do not dare" should be recalled. Some tips collected over the years might help the reader.

It is always good to have a clearer idea of what can be gained. Looking at the subject and the surrounding scene and trying to pre-visualize how to frame, what kind of value and exposure is suitable to use, are quite important factors. More things shalt set in advance and the less time one will need later : timing should be quicker so that the subject will be so pleased with the speed, maybe willing to grant some other shot. Imagine if oneself in front of the camera, while a stranger framing the scene for endless minutes, turning the car, ducking, changing the settings on the SLR, getting up, changing target and then maybe a cool apology. It is not a great feeling.

Nothing there of apprehensions for having to ask for something unknown and even many times of having to pose another person but the opportunity to concentrate on observing the scene and try to predict the best time to catch a winning image is the key.

The photographed eyes should turned directly towards the photographer, mouth opened with a smile. It is enough to lower the camera for a second thought because : after you have finished you will see the lost casual glance, which is more natural and true. Other times, we incur the error of not properly evaluating the situation before launching with much conviction. The exercise of observing before approaching a person also serves to determine the most appropriate time to approach the subject.

16 TIPS FOR BEAUTIFUL BACKGROUND

They are beautiful on the Christmas tree or in the elaborated designs that adorn the city streets and shops; it is quite common to find oneself in such situations.

If there was one thing – Christmas Tree, for that many always liked to die – Christmas is an occasion which actually is not bound by any religion, the reason are the lights, they move and are colorful, what one can want more?

These lights are beautiful on the Christmas tree, on the houses or in the elaborate designs that adorn the city streets and shops. As it happens, all this beauty lends itself to the creation of photo definitely fascinating. Almost everyone set up a Christmas tree in the house, now have a subject who is always available...

In the same way, Diwali in India is a Mega version of Christmas – if the reader is not aware of, search with "Images for diwali night india" in Google search.

For Christmas or Diwali, a good idea is to photograph people in the act of decorating the related materials. In this way, the photos will tell a story, avoid capturing an object. On the houses or in the elaborate designs that adorn the city streets and shops. Bokeh is a Japanese term that is often used to indicate the focus. These lights are suitable for creating a blurred, interesting background. Custom Bokeh shapes are sold, combining can result great creation.

As the shooting will be under very low lighting situation, here are some tips :

Placing the camera on a tripod
Disabling the image stabilization
If possible, setting up the lights in a manner so that they remain in either constantly lit or blinking very frequently mode
Choosing the aperture priority (A or Av) mode
Setting the mode of exposure measurement to matrix or evaluative
Setting the ISO to minimum
Choosing a larger aperture will ensure a better depth of field
Using a delayed shutter release or remote control to shoot

In this way, the camera should be able to calculate a balanced exposure, automatically. There may be, however, several exceptions.

First, if one do not have the opportunity to keep switching on the lights to ON state, flashing or blinking might fool the automatic calculation of exposure. Secondly, the camera may tend to underexpose to avoid burning out the lights. In both cases, the best solution is to resort to manual mode. This means that one must proceed as described above, but in addition you must also adjust the shutter speed.

Then doing the following will solve the problems :

Setting everything up as described above (except the shooting mode, which will be manual)
Adjusting the exposure time in order to obtain balanced exposure
Taking a test shot

If the photo is underexposed, increasing the time or else reducing should fix the problem.

In fact, if one can not keep the lights fixed, blinking lights may turn off right in the moment of shots. To make sure to have all the lights ON in the picture, just lengthening the exposure time will work - all lights will be glowing at least once in the meantime when the shutter is open. A longer time will also allow the lights to be more intense.

Obviously, for the rules of the exposure triangle will play, if one is trying to increase the shutter speed too much, he/she is taking the risk of overexposing. In this case, the solution is to increase the aperture value. Of course, it increases the depth of field and reduce the blur. At this point one will have to make a choice, as often happens between exposure and focus.

ABOUT THE AUTHOR

Dr. Abhishek Ghosh, MD/MS (Orthopedics), PhD (Student) is an Indian technology blog publisher since the past 5 years with a royal, business family background. He created a genre of blog which existed on the West with regular self publication of articles on core technology.

The revenue generated from this book will be donated to the charity after paying the income tax like his other earnings are donated. You are encouraged to contact him for any topic related to this book. You are discouraged to contact him for other reasons.

www.ingramcontent.com/pod-product-compliance
Lightning Source LLC
Chambersburg PA
CBHW021416170526
45164CB00002B/667